MznLnx

Missing Links Exam Preps

Exam Prep for

Trigonometry

McKeague, Turner, 5th Edition

The MznLnx Exam Prep is your link from the texbook and lecture to your exams.
The MznLnx Exam Preps are unauthorized and comprehensive reviews of your textbooks.

All material provided by MznLnx and Rico Publications (c) 2010
Textbook publishers and textbook authors do not particpate in or contribute to these reviews.

MznLnx

Rico Publications

Exam Prep for Trigonometry
5th Edition
McKeague, Turner

Publisher: Raymond Houge
Assistant Editor: Michael Rouger
Text and Cover Designer: Lisa Buckner
Marketing Manager: Sara Swagger
Project Manager, Editorial Production: Jerry Emerson
Art Director: Vernon Lowerui

Product Manager: Dave Mason
Editorial Assitant: Rachel Guzmanji
Pedagogy: Debra Long
Cover Image: Jim Reed/Getty Images
Text and Cover Printer: City Printing, Inc.
Compositor: Media Mix, Inc.

(c) 2010 Rico Publications
ALL RIGHTS RESERVED. No part of this work covered by the copyright may be reproduced or used in any form or by an means--graphic, electronic, or mechanical, including photocopying, recording, taping, Web distribution, information storage, and retrieval systems, or in any other manner--without the written permission of the publisher.

Printed in the United States
ISBN:

For more information about our products, contact us at:
Dave.Mason@RicoPublications.com

For permission to use material from this text or product, submit a request online to:
Dave.Mason@RicoPublications.com

Contents

CHAPTER 1
THE SIX TRIGONOMETRIC FUNCTIONS — 1

CHAPTER 2
RIGHT TRIANGLE TRIGONOMETRY — 13

CHAPTER 3
RADIAN MEASURE — 20

CHAPTER 4
GRAPHING AND INVERSE FUNCTIONS — 27

CHAPTER 5
IDENTITIES AND FORMULAS — 31

CHAPTER 6
EQUATIONS — 33

CHAPTER 7
TRIANGLES — 36

CHAPTER 8
COMPLEX NUMBERS AND POLAR COORDINATES — 41

ANSWER KEY — 50

TO THE STUDENT

COMPREHENSIVE

The *MznLnx* Exam Prep series is designed to help you pass your exams. Editors at MznLnx review your textbooks and then prepare these practice exams to help you master the textbook material. Unlike study guides, workbooks, and practice tests provided by the texbook publisher and textbook authors, *MznLnx* gives you **all** of the material in each chapter in exam form, not just samples, so you can be sure to nail your exam.

MECHANICAL

The MznLnx Exam Prep series creates exams that will help you learn the subject matter as well as test you on your understanding. Each question is designed to help you master the concept. Just working through the exams, you gain an understanding of the subject--its a simple mechanical process that produces success.

INTEGRATED STUDY GUIDE AND REVIEW

MznLnx is not just a set of exams designed to test you, its also a comprehensive review of the subject content. Each exam question is also a review of the concept, making sure that you will get the answer correct without having to go to other sources of material. You learn as you go! Its the easiest way to pass an exam.

HUMOR

Studying can be tedious and dry. MznLnx's instructional design includes moderate humor within the exam questions on occassion, to break the tedium and revitalize the brain

Chapter 1. THE SIX TRIGONOMETRIC FUNCTIONS

1. In geometry and trigonometry, an _____ is the figure formed by two rays sharing a common endpoint, called the vertex of the _____ . The magnitude of the _____ is the 'amount of rotation' that separates the two rays, and can be measured by considering the length of circular arc swept out when one ray is rotated about the vertex to coincide with the other Where there is no possibility of confusion, the term '_____' is used interchangeably for both the geometric configuration itself and for its angular magnitude (which is simply a numerical quantity.)
    a. Additive identity
    b. Affinely extended real number system
    c. Angle
    d. Absolute value

2. A pair of angles are complementary if the sum of their measures is 90 degrees.

If the two _____ are adjacent (i.e. have a common vertex and share just one side) their non-shared sides form a right angle.

In Euclidean geometry, the two acute angles in a right triangle are complementary, because the sum of internal angles of a triangle is 180 degrees, and the right angle itself accounts for ninety degrees.

    a. Complementary angles
    b. Belt problem
    c. Best fit
    d. Line

3. A convention universally adopted in mathematical writing is that angles given a sign are positive angles if measured anticlockwise, and _____s if measured clockwise, from a given line. If no line is specified, it can be assumed to be the x-axis in the Cartesian plane. In many geometrical situations a _____ of −θ is effectively equivalent to a positive angle of 'one full rotation less θ'.
    a. Belt problem
    b. Negative angle
    c. Best fit
    d. Bounded

4. A convention universally adopted in mathematical writing is that angles given a sign are _____s if measured anticlockwise, and negative angles if measured clockwise, from a given line. If no line is specified, it can be assumed to be the x-axis in the Cartesian plane. In many geometrical situations a negative angle of −θ is effectively equivalent to a _____ of 'one full rotation less θ'.

Chapter 1. THE SIX TRIGONOMETRIC FUNCTIONS

   a. Positive angle
   b. Best fit
   c. Belt problem
   d. Bounded

5. In geometry and trigonometry, a _____ is an angle of 90 degrees, corresponding to a quarter turn (that is, a quarter of a full circle.) It can be defined as the angle such that twice that angle amounts to a half turn, or 180°.

Lines that are at a _____ to each other are perpendicular, an important geometrical property.

   a. Belt problem
   b. Best fit
   c. Right angle
   d. Bounded

6. _____ are pairs of angles whose measures add up to 180 degrees. If the two _____ are adjacent (i.e. have a common vertex and share just one side), their non-shared sides form a line. The supplement of an angle of 135 degrees is an angle of 45 degrees.
   a. Best fit
   b. Belt problem
   c. Bounded
   d. Supplementary angles

7. A _____ is the longest side of a right triangle, the side opposite the right angle. The length of the _____ of a right triangle can be found using the Pythagorean theorem, which states that the square of the length of the _____ equals the sum of the squares of the lengths of the other two sides.

For example, if one of the other sides has a length of 3 meters (when squared, 9 m^2) and the other has a length of 4 m (when squared, 16 m^2.)

   a. Best fit
   b. Belt problem
   c. Bounded
   d. Hypotenuse

8. A _____ or right-angled triangle is a triangle in which one angle is a right angle (that is, a 90 degree angle.)

The side opposite the right angle is called the hypotenuse (side [BC] in the figure above.) The sides adjacent to the right angle are called legs or catheti (singular: cathetus.)

a. Right triangle
b. Bounded
c. Belt problem
d. Best fit

9. A _____ is a right triangle with some regular feature that makes calculations on the triangle easier, or for which simple formulas exist. For example, a right triangle may have angles that form a simple ratio, such as 45-45-90. This is called an 'angle based' right triangle.
a. Belt problem
b. Special right triangle
c. Bounded
d. Best fit

10. A _____ is one of the basic shapes of geometry: a polygon with three corners or vertices and three sides or edges which are line segments. A _____ with vertices A, B, and C is denoted ABC.

In Euclidean geometry any three non-collinear points determine a unique _____ and a unique plane (i.e. a two-dimensional Euclidean space.)

a. Belt problem
b. Bounded
c. Best fit
d. Triangle

11. In mathematics, the _____ or Pythagoras' theorem is a relation in Euclidean geometry among the three sides of a right triangle . It states:

In any right triangle, the area of the square whose side is the hypotenuse (the side opposite the right angle) is equal to the sum of the areas of the squares whose sides are the two legs (the two sides that meet at a right angle.)

The theorem can be written as an equation:

$$a^2 + b^2 = c^2$$

where c represents the length of the hypotenuse, and a and b represent the lengths of the other two sides.

a. Bounded
b. Best fit
c. Belt problem
d. Pythagorean theorem

12. A _____ consists of three positive integers a, b, and c, such that $a^2 + b^2 = c^2$. Such a triple is commonly written (a, b, c), and a well-known example is (3, 4, 5). If (a, b, c) is a _____, then so is (ka, kb, kc) for any positive integer k.

a. Pythagorean triple
b. Belt problem
c. Bounded
d. Best fit

13. Pythagoreanism is a term used for the esoteric and metaphysical beliefs held by Pythagoras and his followers, the _____, who were much influenced by mathematics and probably a very inspirational source for Plato and Platonism. Later resurgence of ideas similar to those held by the early _____ are collected under the term Neopythagoreanism.

According to tradition, Pythagoreanism developed at some point into two separate schools of thought, the akousmatikoi ('listeners') and the mathÄ"matikoi ('learners'.)

a. Best fit
b. Bounded
c. Belt problem
d. Pythagoreans

14. In mathematics, a _____ specifies each point uniquely in a plane by a pair of numerical coordinates, which are the signed distances from the point to two fixed perpendicular directed lines, measured in the same unit of length.

Each reference line is called a coordinate axis or just axis of the system, and the point where they meet is its origin. The coordinates can also be defined as the positions of the perpendicular projections of the point onto the two axes, expressed as a signed distances from the origin.

a. Cartesian coordinate system
b. Best fit
c. Belt problem
d. Bounded

Chapter 1. THE SIX TRIGONOMETRIC FUNCTIONS 5

15. In informal usage, _____ systems can have singularities: these are points where one or more of the _____s is not well-defined. For example, the origin in the polar _____ system (r,θ) on the plane is singular, because although the radial _____ has a well-defined value (r = 0) at the origin, θ can be any angle, and so is not a well-defined function at the origin. The Cartesian _____ system in the plane.

The prototypical example of a _____ system is the Cartesian _____ system, which describes the position of a point P in the Euclidean space R^n by an n-tuple

$P = (r_1, ..., r_n)$

of real numbers

$r_1, ..., r_n.$

a. Belt problem
b. Best fit
c. Bounded
d. Coordinate

16. In mathematics, an _____ is a collection of objects having two coordinates (or entries or projections), such that one can always uniquely determine the object, which is the first coordinate (or first entry or left projection) of the pair as well as the second coordinate (or second entry or right projection.) If the first coordinate is a and the second is b, the usual notation for an _____ is (a, b.) The pair is 'ordered' in that (a, b) differs from (b, a) unless a = b.
a. Additive identity
b. Ordered pair
c. Affinely extended real number system
d. Absolute value

17. _____, usually called coordinate geometry and earlier referred to as Cartesian geometry or analytical geometry, is the study of geometry using the principles of algebra; the modern development of _____ is thus suggestively called algebraic geometry.

Usually the Cartesian coordinate system is applied to manipulate equations for planes, straight lines, and squares, often in two and sometimes in three dimensions of measurement. Geometrically, one studies the Euclidean plane (2 dimensions) and Euclidean space (3 dimensions.)

Chapter 1. THE SIX TRIGONOMETRIC FUNCTIONS

a. Additive identity
b. Absolute value
c. Affinely extended real number system
d. Analytic geometry

18. _____ is a part of mathematics concerned with questions of size, shape, and relative position of figures and with properties of space. _____ is one of the oldest sciences. Initially a body of practical knowledge concerning lengths, areas, and volumes, in the third century BC _____ was put into an axiomatic form by Euclid, whose treatment--Euclidean _____--set a standard for many centuries to follow.
   a. Best fit
   b. Belt problem
   c. Bounded
   d. Geometry

19. In mathematics, a _____ is a circle with a unit radius, i.e., a circle whose radius is 1. Frequently, especially in trigonometry, 'the' _____ is the circle of radius 1 centered at the origin (0, 0) in the Cartesian coordinate system in the Euclidean plane. The _____ is often denoted S^1; the generalization to higher dimensions is the unit sphere.
   a. Additive identity
   b. Affinely extended real number system
   c. Absolute value
   d. Unit circle

20. A _____ is a simple shape of Euclidean geometry consisting of those points in a plane which are the same distance from a given point called the centre. The common distance of the points of a _____ from its center is called its radius.

   _____s are simple closed curves which divide the plane into two regions, an interior and an exterior.

   a. Belt problem
   b. Bounded
   c. Best fit
   d. Circle

21. In category theory, an abstract branch of mathematics, an _____ of a category C is an object I in C such that for every object X in C, there exists precisely one morphism I → X. The dual notion is that of a terminal object (also called terminal element): T is terminal if for every object X in C there exists a single morphism X → T. _____s are also called coterminal or universal, and terminal objects are also called final.

Chapter 1. THE SIX TRIGONOMETRIC FUNCTIONS

If an object is both initial and terminal, it is called a zero object or null object.

- The empty set is the unique _____ in the category of sets; every one-element set (singleton) is a terminal object in this category; there are no zero objects.
- Similarly, the empty space is the unique _____ in the category of topological spaces; every one-point space is a terminal object in this category.
- In the category of non-empty sets, there are no _____ s. The singletons are not initial: while every non-empty set admits a function from a singleton, this function is in general not unique.
- In the category of groups, any trivial group is a zero object. The same is true for the categories of abelian groups, modules over a ring, and vector spaces over a field. This is the origin of the term 'zero object'.
- In the category of semigroups, the empty semigroup is an _____ and any singleton semigroup is a terminal object. There are no zero objects. In the subcategory of monoids, however, every trivial monoid (consisting of only the identity element) is a zero object.
- In the category of pointed sets (whose objects are non-empty sets together with a distinguished element; a morphism from (A,a) to (B,b) being a function f : A → B with f(a) = b), every singleton is a zero object. Similarly, in the category of pointed topological spaces, every singleton is a zero object.
- In the category of rings with unity and unity-perserving morphisms, the ring of integers Z is an _____. The trivial ring consisting only of a single element 0=1 is a terminal object. In the category of general rings with homomorphisms, the trivial ring is a zero object.
- In the category of fields, there are no initial or terminal objects. However, in the subcategory of fields of characteristic p, the prime field of characteristic p forms an _____.
- Any partially ordered set (P, ≤) can be interpreted as a category: the objects are the elements of P, and there is a single morphism from x to y if and only if x ≤ y. This category has an _____ if and only if P has a least element; it has a terminal object if and only if P has a greatest element.
- If a monoid is considered as a category with a single object, this object is neither initial or terminal unless the monoid is trivial, in which case it is both.
- In the category of graphs, the null graph (without vertices and edges) is an _____. The graph with a single vertex and a single loop is terminal. The category of simple graphs does not have a terminal object.
- Similarly, the category of all small categories with functors as morphisms has the empty category as _____ and the category 1 (with a single object and morphism) as terminal object.
- Any topological space X can be viewed as a category by taking the open sets as objects, and a single morphism between two open sets U and V if and only if U ⊂ V. The empty set is the _____ of this category, and X is the terminal object. This is a special case of the case 'partially ordered set', mentioned above. Take P:= the set of open subsets
- If X is a topological space (viewed as a category as above) and C is some small category, we can form the category of all contravariant functors from X to C, using natural transformations as morphisms. This category is called the category of presheaves on X with values in C. If C has an _____ c, then the constant functor which sends every open set to c is an _____ in the category of presheaves. Similarly, if C has a terminal object, then the corresponding constant functor serves as a terminal presheaf.
- In the category of schemes, Spec(Z) the prime spectrum of the ring of integers is a terminal object. The empty scheme (equal to the prime spectrum of the trivial ring) is an _____.
- If we fix a homomorphism f : A → B of abelian groups, we can consider the category C consisting of all pairs (X, φ) where X is an abelian group and φ : X → A is a group homomorphism with f φ = 0. A morphism from the pair (X, φ) to the pair (Y, ψ) is defined to be a group homomorphism r : X → Y with the property ψ r = φ. The kernel of f is a terminal object in this category; this is nothing but a reformulation of the universal property of kernels. With an analogous construction, the cokernel of f can be seen as an _____ of a suitable category.
- In the category of interpretations of an algebraic model, the _____ is the initial algebra, the interpretation that provides as many distinct objects as the model allows and no more.

Chapter 1. THE SIX TRIGONOMETRIC FUNCTIONS

Initial and terminal objects are not required to exist in a given category. However, if they do exist, they are essentially unique.

    a. Additive identity
    b. Absolute value
    c. Affinely extended real number system
    d. Initial object

22. The _____ csc(A) is the reciprocal of sin(A), i.e. the ratio of the length of the hypotenuse to the length of the opposite side:

$$\csc A = \frac{\text{hypotenuse}}{\text{opposite}} = \frac{h}{a}.$$

The secant sec(A) is the reciprocal of cos(A), i.e. the ratio of the length of the hypotenuse to the length of the adjacent side:

$$\sec A = \frac{\text{hypotenuse}}{\text{adjacent}} = \frac{h}{b}.$$

The cotangent cot(A) is the reciprocal of tan(A), i.e. the ratio of the length of the adjacent side to the length of the opposite side:

$$\cot A = \frac{\text{adjacent}}{\text{opposite}} = \frac{b}{a}.$$

Equivalent to the right-triangle definitions the trigonometric functions can be defined in terms of the rise, run, and slope of a line segment relative to some horizontal line. The slope is commonly taught as 'rise over run' or rise/run. The three main trigonometric functions are commonly taught in the order sine, cosine, tangent.

    a. Bounded
    b. Belt problem
    c. Best fit
    d. Cosecant

23. The _____ of an angle is the ratio of the length of the adjacent side to the length of the hypotenuse. In our case

$$\cos A = \frac{\text{adjacent}}{\text{hypotenuse}} = \frac{b}{h}.$$

The tangent of an angle is the ratio of the length of the opposite side to the length of the adjacent side. In our case

$$\tan A = \frac{\text{opposite}}{\text{adjacent}} = \frac{a}{b}.$$

The remaining three functions are best defined using the above three functions.

a. Best fit
b. Belt problem
c. Bounded
d. Cosine

24. The _____ cot(A) is the reciprocal of tan(A), i.e. the ratio of the length of the adjacent side to the length of the opposite side:

$$\cot A = \frac{\text{adjacent}}{\text{opposite}} = \frac{b}{a}.$$

Equivalent to the right-triangle definitions the trigonometric functions can be defined in terms of the rise, run, and slope of a line segment relative to some horizontal line. The slope is commonly taught as 'rise over run' or rise/run. The three main trigonometric functions are commonly taught in the order sine, cosine, tangent.

a. Bounded
b. Cotangent
c. Belt problem
d. Best fit

25. The mathematical concept of a _____ expresses the intuitive idea that one quantity completely determines another quantity A _____ associates a unique value for each input of a specified type. The argument and value may be real numbers, but they can also be elements from any given sets: the domain and codomain of the _____.

Chapter 1. THE SIX TRIGONOMETRIC FUNCTIONS

a. Belt problem
b. Function
c. Bounded
d. Best fit

26. The _____ of an angle is the ratio of the length of the opposite side to the length of the hypotenuse. In our case

$$\sin A = \frac{\text{opposite}}{\text{hypotenuse}} = \frac{a}{h}.$$

Note that this ratio does not depend on size of the particular right triangle chosen, as long as it contains the angle A, since all such triangles are similar.

The cosine of an angle is the ratio of the length of the adjacent side to the length of the hypotenuse.

a. Best fit
b. Belt problem
c. Bounded
d. Sine

27. In geometry, the _____ line (or simply the _____) to a curve at a given point is the straight line that 'just touches' the curve at that point (in the sense explained more precisely below.) As it passes through the point of tangency, the _____ line is 'going in the same direction' as the curve, and in this sense it is the best straight-line approximation to the curve at that point. The same definition applies to space curves and curves in n-dimensional Euclidean space.

a. Best fit
b. Bounded
c. Belt problem
d. Tangent

28. Trigonometry is a branch of mathematics that deals with triangles, particularly those plane triangles in which one angle has 90 degrees (right triangles.) Trigonometry deals with relationships between the sides and the angles of triangles and with the _____ functions, which describe those relationships.

Trigonometry has applications in both pure mathematics and in applied mathematics, where it is essential in many branches of science and technology.

a. Bounded
b. Belt problem
c. Trigonometric
d. Best fit

29. In mathematics, the _____ are functions of an angle. They are used to relate the angles of a triangle to the lengths of the sides of a triangle. _____ are important in the study of triangles and modeling periodic phenomena, among many other applications.
   a. Law of sines
   b. Law of cosines
   c. Law of tangents
   d. Trigonometric functions

30. In mathematics, the term _____ has several different important meanings:

- An _____ is an equality that remains true regardless of the values of any variables that appear within it, to distinguish it from an equality which is true under more particular conditions. For this, the 'triple bar' symbol ≡ is sometimes used. (However, this can be ambiguous since the same symbol can also be used with different meanings, for example for a congruence relation.)
- In algebra, an _____ or _____ element of a set S with a binary operation Â· is an element e that, when combined with any element x of S, produces that same x. That is, eÂ·x = xÂ·e = x for all x in S.
   - The _____ function from a set S to itself, often denoted id or id_S, is the function such that id(x) = x for all x in S. This function serves as the _____ element in the set of all functions from S to itself with respect to function composition.
   - In linear algebra, the _____ matrix of size n is the n-by-n square matrix with ones on the main diagonal and zeros elsewhere. This matrix serves as the _____ with respect to matrix multiplication.

A common example of the first meaning is the trigonometric _____

$$\sin^2 \theta + \cos^2 \theta = 1$$

which is true for all complex values of θ (since the complex numbers $\mathbb{C}$ are the domain of sin and cos), as opposed to

$$\cos \theta = 1,$$

which is true only for some values of θ, not all. For example, the latter equation is true when $\theta = 0$, false when $\theta = 2$

The concepts of 'additive _____' and 'multiplicative _____' are central to the Peano axioms. The number 0 is the 'additive _____' for integers, real numbers, and complex numbers. For the real numbers, for all $a \in \mathbb{R}$,

$$0 + a = a,$$

$$a + 0 = a, \text{ and}$$

$$0 + 0 = 0.$$

Similarly, The number 1 is the 'multiplicative _____' for integers, real numbers, and complex numbers.

- a. Affinely extended real number system
- b. Additive identity
- c. Absolute value
- d. Identity

31. In mathematics, _____ are equalities that involve trigonometric functions that are true for every single value of the occurring variables. Geometrically, these are identities involving certain functions of one or more angles. These are distinct from triangle identities, which are identities involving both angles and side lengths of a triangle.
- a. Best fit
- b. Bounded
- c. Belt problem
- d. Trigonometric identities

32. A _____ is an expression that compares quantities relative to each other. The most common examples involve two quantities, but any number of quantities can be compared. _____s are represented mathematically by separating each quantity with a colon, for example the _____ 2:3, which is read as the _____ 'two to three'.
- a. Best fit
- b. Bounded
- c. Belt problem
- d. Ratio

Chapter 2. RIGHT TRIANGLE TRIGONOMETRY

1. A _____ of a function of two variables is a curve along which the function has a constant value. In cartography, a _____ (often just called a 'contour') joins points of equal elevation (height) above a given level, such as mean sea level. A contour map is a map illustrated with _____s, for example a topographic map, which thus shows valleys and hills, and the steepness of slopes.
    a. Contour line
    b. Bounded
    c. Best fit
    d. Belt problem

2. A _____ is a type of map characterized by large-scale detail and quantitative representation of relief, usually using contour lines in modern mapping, but historically using a variety of methods. Traditional definitions require a _____ to show both natural and man-made features.

The Canadian Centre for Topographic Information provides this definition of a _____:

Other authors define _____s by contrasting them with another type of map; they are distinguished from smaller-scale 'chorographic maps' that cover large regions, 'planimetric maps' that do not show elevations, and 'thematic maps' that focus on specific topics.

    a. Best fit
    b. Belt problem
    c. Bounded
    d. Topographic map

3. In Euclidean geometry, a _____ is a straight curve. When geometry is used to model the real world, _____s are used to represent straight objects with negligible width and height. _____s are an idealisation of such objects and have no width or height at all and are usually considered to be infinitely long.
    a. Best fit
    b. Belt problem
    c. Bounded
    d. Line

4. The _____ csc(A) is the reciprocal of sin(A), i.e. the ratio of the length of the hypotenuse to the length of the opposite side:

$$\csc A = \frac{\text{hypotenuse}}{\text{opposite}} = \frac{h}{a}.$$

Chapter 2. RIGHT TRIANGLE TRIGONOMETRY

The secant sec(A) is the reciprocal of cos(A), i.e. the ratio of the length of the hypotenuse to the length of the adjacent side:

$$\sec A = \frac{\text{hypotenuse}}{\text{adjacent}} = \frac{h}{b}.$$

The cotangent cot(A) is the reciprocal of tan(A), i.e. the ratio of the length of the adjacent side to the length of the opposite side:

$$\cot A = \frac{\text{adjacent}}{\text{opposite}} = \frac{b}{a}.$$

Equivalent to the right-triangle definitions the trigonometric functions can be defined in terms of the rise, run, and slope of a line segment relative to some horizontal line. The slope is commonly taught as 'rise over run' or rise/run. The three main trigonometric functions are commonly taught in the order sine, cosine, tangent.

- a. Best fit
- b. Belt problem
- c. Bounded
- d. Cosecant

5. The _____ of an angle is the ratio of the length of the adjacent side to the length of the hypotenuse. In our case

$$\cos A = \frac{\text{adjacent}}{\text{hypotenuse}} = \frac{b}{h}.$$

The tangent of an angle is the ratio of the length of the opposite side to the length of the adjacent side. In our case

$$\tan A = \frac{\text{opposite}}{\text{adjacent}} = \frac{a}{b}.$$

The remaining three functions are best defined using the above three functions.

- a. Cosine
- b. Belt problem
- c. Bounded
- d. Best fit

6. The _____ cot(A) is the reciprocal of tan(A), i.e. the ratio of the length of the adjacent side to the length of the opposite side:

$$\cot A = \frac{\text{adjacent}}{\text{opposite}} = \frac{b}{a}.$$

Equivalent to the right-triangle definitions the trigonometric functions can be defined in terms of the rise, run, and slope of a line segment relative to some horizontal line. The slope is commonly taught as 'rise over run' or rise/run. The three main trigonometric functions are commonly taught in the order sine, cosine, tangent.

   a. Belt problem
   b. Bounded
   c. Best fit
   d. Cotangent

7. The mathematical concept of a _____ expresses the intuitive idea that one quantity completely determines another quantity A _____ associates a unique value for each input of a specified type. The argument and value may be real numbers, but they can also be elements from any given sets: the domain and codomain of the _____.
   a. Belt problem
   b. Bounded
   c. Best fit
   d. Function

8. The _____ of an angle is the ratio of the length of the opposite side to the length of the hypotenuse. In our case

$$\sin A = \frac{\text{opposite}}{\text{hypotenuse}} = \frac{a}{h}.$$

Note that this ratio does not depend on size of the particular right triangle chosen, as long as it contains the angle A, since all such triangles are similar.

The cosine of an angle is the ratio of the length of the adjacent side to the length of the hypotenuse.

   a. Best fit
   b. Bounded
   c. Belt problem
   d. Sine

16   *Chapter 2. RIGHT TRIANGLE TRIGONOMETRY*

9. In geometry, the _____ line (or simply the _____) to a curve at a given point is the straight line that 'just touches' the curve at that point (in the sense explained more precisely below.) As it passes through the point of tangency, the _____ line is 'going in the same direction' as the curve, and in this sense it is the best straight-line approximation to the curve at that point. The same definition applies to space curves and curves in n-dimensional Euclidean space.
   a. Belt problem
   b. Tangent
   c. Best fit
   d. Bounded

10. Trigonometry is a branch of mathematics that deals with triangles, particularly those plane triangles in which one angle has 90 degrees (right triangles.) Trigonometry deals with relationships between the sides and the angles of triangles and with the _____ functions, which describe those relationships.

Trigonometry has applications in both pure mathematics and in applied mathematics, where it is essential in many branches of science and technology.

   a. Best fit
   b. Belt problem
   c. Bounded
   d. Trigonometric

11. In mathematics, the _____ are functions of an angle. They are used to relate the angles of a triangle to the lengths of the sides of a triangle. _____ are important in the study of triangles and modeling periodic phenomena, among many other applications.
   a. Law of cosines
   b. Law of tangents
   c. Trigonometric functions
   d. Law of sines

12. In mathematics, a function f is _____ of a function g if f(A) = g(B) whenever A and B are complementary angles. This definition typically applies to trigonometric functions.

For example, sine and cosine are _____s of each other (hence the 'co' in 'cosine'):

The same is true of secant and cosecant and of tangent and cotangent:

Sometimes writing a function in terms of its _____ helps solve trigonometric equations.

a. Belt problem
b. Cofunction
c. Bounded
d. Best fit

13. In geometry and trigonometry, an _____ is the figure formed by two rays sharing a common endpoint, called the vertex of the _____ . The magnitude of the _____ is the 'amount of rotation' that separates the two rays, and can be measured by considering the length of circular arc swept out when one ray is rotated about the vertex to coincide with the other Where there is no possibility of confusion, the term '_____' is used interchangeably for both the geometric configuration itself and for its angular magnitude (which is simply a numerical quantity.)

a. Additive identity
b. Absolute value
c. Affinely extended real number system
d. Angle

14. A _____ is one of the basic shapes of geometry: a polygon with three corners or vertices and three sides or edges which are line segments. A _____ with vertices A, B, and C is denoted ABC.

In Euclidean geometry any three non-collinear points determine a unique _____ and a unique plane (i.e. a two-dimensional Euclidean space.)

a. Best fit
b. Bounded
c. Triangle
d. Belt problem

15. The _____ of a geographic location is its height above a fixed reference point, often the mean sea level. _____, or geometric height, is mainly used when referring to points on the Earth's surface, while altitude or geopotential height is used for points above the surface, such as an aircraft in flight or a spacecraft in orbit.

Less commonly, _____ is measured using the center of the Earth as the reference point.

a. Affinely extended real number system
b. Absolute value
c. Additive identity
d. Elevation

16. In mathematics, the _____ of two monic polynomials P and Q over a field k is defined as the product

$$\mathrm{res}(P,Q) = \prod_{(x,y):\, P(x)=0,\, Q(y)=0} (x-y),$$

of the differences of their roots, where x and y take on values in the algebraic closure of k. For non-monic polynomials with leading coefficients p and q, respectively, the above product is multiplied by

$$p^{\deg Q} q^{\deg P}.$$

- The _____ is the determinant of the Sylvester matrix (and of the Bezout matrix.)

- When Q is separable, the above product can be rewritten to

$$\mathrm{res}(P,Q) = \prod_{P(x)=0} Q(x)$$

and this expression remains unchanged if Q is reduced modulo P. Note that, when non-monic, this includes the factor $q^{\deg P}$ but still needs the factor $p^{\deg Q}$.

- Let $P' = P \mod Q$. The above idea can be continued by swapping the roles of P' and Q. However, P' has a set of roots different from that of P. This can be resolved by writing $\prod_{Q(y)=0} P'(y)$ as a determinant again, where P' has leading zero coefficients. This determinant can now be simplified by iterative expansion with respect to the column, where only the leading coefficient q of Q appears.

$$\mathrm{res}(P,Q) = q^{\deg P - \deg P'} \cdot \mathrm{res}(P',Q)$$

Continuing this procedure ends up in a variant of the Euclidean algorithm. This procedure needs quadratic runtime.

a. Bounded
b. Best fit
c. Belt problem
d. Resultant

17. A standard definition of _____ is:

A system of particles is in _____ when all the particles of the system are at rest and the total force on each particle is permanently zero.

This is a strict definition, and often the term '_____' is used in a more relaxed manner interchangeably with 'mechanical equilibrium', as defined next.

A standard definition of mechanical equilibrium for a particle is:

> The necessary and sufficient conditions for a particle to be in mechanical equilibrium is that the net force acting upon the particle is zero.

a. Belt problem
b. Bounded
c. Best fit
d. Static equilibrium

Chapter 3. RADIAN MEASURE

1. In geometry and trigonometry, an _____ is the figure formed by two rays sharing a common endpoint, called the vertex of the _____ . The magnitude of the _____ is the 'amount of rotation' that separates the two rays, and can be measured by considering the length of circular arc swept out when one ray is rotated about the vertex to coincide with the other Where there is no possibility of confusion, the term '_____' is used interchangeably for both the geometric configuration itself and for its angular magnitude (which is simply a numerical quantity.)
    a. Angle
    b. Additive identity
    c. Absolute value
    d. Affinely extended real number system

2. The _____ is a unit of plane angle, equal to 180/π (or 360/2π) degrees or about 57°17′45″. It is the standard unit of angular measurement in all areas of mathematics beyond the elementary level.

    The _____ is represented by the symbol 'rad' or, more rarely, by the superscript c (for 'circular measure'.)

    a. Belt problem
    b. Bounded
    c. Best fit
    d. Radian

3. In mathematics, a _____ is a circle with a unit radius, i.e., a circle whose radius is 1. Frequently, especially in trigonometry, 'the' _____ is the circle of radius 1 centered at the origin (0, 0) in the Cartesian coordinate system in the Euclidean plane. The _____ is often denoted S^1; the generalization to higher dimensions is the unit sphere.
    a. Additive identity
    b. Unit circle
    c. Affinely extended real number system
    d. Absolute value

4. A _____ is a simple shape of Euclidean geometry consisting of those points in a plane which are the same distance from a given point called the centre. The common distance of the points of a _____ from its center is called its radius.

    _____s are simple closed curves which divide the plane into two regions, an interior and an exterior.

    a. Bounded
    b. Belt problem
    c. Best fit
    d. Circle

Chapter 3. RADIAN MEASURE

5. In mathematics, the _____ are functions of an angle. They are used to relate the angles of a triangle to the lengths of the sides of a triangle. _____ are important in the study of triangles and modeling periodic phenomena, among many other applications.
   a. Law of cosines
   b. Law of sines
   c. Law of tangents
   d. Trigonometric functions

6. The _____ csc(A) is the reciprocal of sin(A), i.e. the ratio of the length of the hypotenuse to the length of the opposite side:

$$\csc A = \frac{\text{hypotenuse}}{\text{opposite}} = \frac{h}{a}.$$

The secant sec(A) is the reciprocal of cos(A), i.e. the ratio of the length of the hypotenuse to the length of the adjacent side:

$$\sec A = \frac{\text{hypotenuse}}{\text{adjacent}} = \frac{h}{b}.$$

The cotangent cot(A) is the reciprocal of tan(A), i.e. the ratio of the length of the adjacent side to the length of the opposite side:

$$\cot A = \frac{\text{adjacent}}{\text{opposite}} = \frac{b}{a}.$$

Equivalent to the right-triangle definitions the trigonometric functions can be defined in terms of the rise, run, and slope of a line segment relative to some horizontal line. The slope is commonly taught as 'rise over run' or rise/run. The three main trigonometric functions are commonly taught in the order sine, cosine, tangent.

   a. Best fit
   b. Bounded
   c. Belt problem
   d. Cosecant

7. The _____ of an angle is the ratio of the length of the adjacent side to the length of the hypotenuse. In our case

$$\cos A = \frac{\text{adjacent}}{\text{hypotenuse}} = \frac{b}{h}.$$

The tangent of an angle is the ratio of the length of the opposite side to the length of the adjacent side. In our case

$$\tan A = \frac{\text{opposite}}{\text{adjacent}} = \frac{a}{b}.$$

The remaining three functions are best defined using the above three functions.

a. Belt problem
b. Bounded
c. Best fit
d. Cosine

8. The _____ cot(A) is the reciprocal of tan(A), i.e. the ratio of the length of the adjacent side to the length of the opposite side:

$$\cot A = \frac{\text{adjacent}}{\text{opposite}} = \frac{b}{a}.$$

Equivalent to the right-triangle definitions the trigonometric functions can be defined in terms of the rise, run, and slope of a line segment relative to some horizontal line. The slope is commonly taught as 'rise over run' or rise/run. The three main trigonometric functions are commonly taught in the order sine, cosine, tangent.

a. Best fit
b. Belt problem
c. Bounded
d. Cotangent

9. The mathematical concept of a _____ expresses the intuitive idea that one quantity completely determines another quantity A _____ associates a unique value for each input of a specified type. The argument and value may be real numbers, but they can also be elements from any given sets: the domain and codomain of the _____.

a. Bounded
b. Function
c. Belt problem
d. Best fit

10. The _____ of an angle is the ratio of the length of the opposite side to the length of the hypotenuse. In our case

$$\sin A = \frac{\text{opposite}}{\text{hypotenuse}} = \frac{a}{h}.$$

Note that this ratio does not depend on size of the particular right triangle chosen, as long as it contains the angle A, since all such triangles are similar.

The cosine of an angle is the ratio of the length of the adjacent side to the length of the hypotenuse.

a. Sine
b. Best fit
c. Belt problem
d. Bounded

11. In geometry, the _____ line (or simply the _____) to a curve at a given point is the straight line that 'just touches' the curve at that point (in the sense explained more precisely below.) As it passes through the point of tangency, the _____ line is 'going in the same direction' as the curve, and in this sense it is the best straight-line approximation to the curve at that point. The same definition applies to space curves and curves in n-dimensional Euclidean space.

a. Belt problem
b. Best fit
c. Bounded
d. Tangent

12. Trigonometry is a branch of mathematics that deals with triangles, particularly those plane triangles in which one angle has 90 degrees (right triangles.) Trigonometry deals with relationships between the sides and the angles of triangles and with the _____ functions, which describe those relationships.

Trigonometry has applications in both pure mathematics and in applied mathematics, where it is essential in many branches of science and technology.

Chapter 3. RADIAN MEASURE

   a. Belt problem
   b. Best fit
   c. Bounded
   d. Trigonometric

13. In mathematics, _____ are a method of defining a curve using parameters. A simple kinematical example is when one uses a time parameter to determine the position, velocity, and other information about a body in motion.

Abstractly, a relation is given in the form of an equation, and it is shown also to be the image of functions from items such as R^n.

   a. Parametric equations
   b. Belt problem
   c. Bounded
   d. Best fit

14. In mathematics, _____s and odd functions are functions which satisfy particular symmetry relations, with respect to taking additive inverses. They are important in many areas of mathematical analysis, especially the theory of power series and Fourier series. They are named for the parity of the powers of the power functions which satisfy each condition: the function f(x) = x^n is an _____ if n is an even integer, and it is an odd function if n is an odd integer.
   a. Absolute value
   b. Odd function
   c. Additive identity
   d. Even function

15. In mathematics, even functions and _____s are functions which satisfy particular symmetry relations, with respect to taking additive inverses. They are important in many areas of mathematical analysis, especially the theory of power series and Fourier series. They are named for the parity of the powers of the power functions which satisfy each condition: the function f(x) = x^n is an even function if n is an even integer, and it is an _____ if n is an odd integer.
   a. Odd function
   b. Absolute value
   c. Affinely extended real number system
   d. Additive identity

16. For some curves there is a smallest number L that is an upper bound on the length of any polygonal approximation. If such a number exists, then the curve is said to be rectifiable and the curve is defined to have _____ L.

Chapter 3. RADIAN MEASURE

Let C be a curve in Euclidean (or, more generally, a metric) space $X = R^n$, so C is the image of a continuous function $f : [a, b] \to X$ of the interval [a, b] into X.

From a partition $a = t_0 < t_1 < ... < t_{n-1} < t_n = b$ of the interval [a, b] we obtain a finite collection of points $f(t_0), f(t_1), ..., f(t_{n-1}), f(t_n)$ on the curve C. Denote the distance from $f(t_i)$ to $f(t_{i+1})$ by $d(f(t_i), f(t_{i+1}))$, which is the length of the line segment connecting the two points.

a. Affinely extended real number system
b. Arc length
c. Absolute value
d. Additive identity

17. The _____ of an object as seen from a given position is the 'visual diameter' of the object measured as an angle. In the vision sciences it is called the visual angle. The visual diameter is the diameter of the perspective projection of the object on a plane through its centre that is perpendicular to the viewing direction.

a. Interior angle
b. Absolute value
c. Additive identity
d. Angular diameter

18. In physics, _____ is defined as the rate of change of position. It is a vector physical quantity; both speed and direction are required to define it. In the SI (metric) system, it is measured in meters per second: (m/s) or ms^{-1}.

a. Bounded
b. Best fit
c. Velocity
d. Belt problem

19. In geometry, a _____ of a circle is any straight line segment that passes through the center of the circle and whose endpoints are on the circle. The _____s are the longest chords of the circle. The word '_____' derives from Greek δι¬μετρος , 'diagonal of a circle', from δια- (dia-), 'across, through' + μÎτρον (metron), 'a measure'.)

a. Bounded
b. Belt problem
c. Best fit
d. Diameter

20. In physics, the _____ is a vector quantity (more precisely, a pseudovector) which specifies the angular speed of an object and the axis about which the object is rotating. The SI unit of _____ is radians per second, although it may be measured in other units such as degrees per second, revolutions per second, degrees per hour, etc. When measured in cycles or rotations per unit time (e.g. revolutions per minute), it is often called the rotational velocity and its magnitude the rotational speed.
   a. Angular velocity
   b. Additive identity
   c. Amplitude
   d. Absolute value

21. Conversion of units refers to _____ between different units of measurement for the same quantity.

The process of making a conversion cannot produce a more precise result than the original quoted figure. Appropriate rounding of results is normally performed after conversion.

   a. Decibel
   b. Conversion factors
   c. Best fit
   d. Belt problem

Chapter 4. GRAPHING AND INVERSE FUNCTIONS

1. In mathematics, a _____ is a circle with a unit radius, i.e., a circle whose radius is 1. Frequently, especially in trigonometry, 'the' _____ is the circle of radius 1 centered at the origin (0, 0) in the Cartesian coordinate system in the Euclidean plane. The _____ is often denoted S^1; the generalization to higher dimensions is the unit sphere.
   a. Additive identity
   b. Unit circle
   c. Affinely extended real number system
   d. Absolute value

2. A _____ is a simple shape of Euclidean geometry consisting of those points in a plane which are the same distance from a given point called the centre. The common distance of the points of a _____ from its center is called its radius.

   _____s are simple closed curves which divide the plane into two regions, an interior and an exterior.

   a. Best fit
   b. Belt problem
   c. Bounded
   d. Circle

3. _____ is the magnitude of change in the oscillating variable, with each oscillation, within an oscillating system. For instance, sound waves are oscillations in atmospheric pressure and their _____s are proportional to the change in pressure during one oscillation. If the variable undergoes regular oscillations, and a graph of the system is drawn with the oscillating variable as the vertical axis and time as the horizontal axis, the _____ is visually represented by the vertical distance between the extrema of the curve.
   a. Angular velocity
   b. Absolute value
   c. Additive identity
   d. Amplitude

4. In geometry, an _____ of a curve is a way of describing its behavior far away from the origin by comparing it to another curve. Specifically, the second curve is an _____ of the first if distance between the two approaches 0 as the points being considered tend to infinity. Informally, this means that the first curve gets closer to the second as it gets farther from the origin.
   a. Affinely extended real number system
   b. Additive identity
   c. Absolute value
   d. Asymptote

Chapter 4. GRAPHING AND INVERSE FUNCTIONS

5. A _____, in mathematics, is a number comprising a real number part and an imaginary number part; it is normally written in the form a + bi, where a and b are real numbers, and i is the square root of minus one.

_____s are a field in mathematics, with specific notions of addition, subtraction, multiplication and division, satisfying certain axioms. These operations extend the corresponding operations on real numbers, mainly because the product of two imaginary numbers (or the square of one imaginary number) is a negative real number.

  a. Best fit
  b. Belt problem
  c. Bounded
  d. Complex number

6. The mathematical concept of a _____ expresses the intuitive idea that one quantity completely determines another quantity A _____ associates a unique value for each input of a specified type. The argument and value may be real numbers, but they can also be elements from any given sets: the domain and codomain of the _____.
  a. Best fit
  b. Bounded
  c. Belt problem
  d. Function

7. Trigonometry is a branch of mathematics that deals with triangles, particularly those plane triangles in which one angle has 90 degrees (right triangles.) Trigonometry deals with relationships between the sides and the angles of triangles and with the _____ functions, which describe those relationships.

Trigonometry has applications in both pure mathematics and in applied mathematics, where it is essential in many branches of science and technology.

  a. Bounded
  b. Belt problem
  c. Trigonometric
  d. Best fit

8. In mathematics, the _____ are functions of an angle. They are used to relate the angles of a triangle to the lengths of the sides of a triangle. _____ are important in the study of triangles and modeling periodic phenomena, among many other applications.

Chapter 4. GRAPHING AND INVERSE FUNCTIONS

a. Law of cosines
b. Law of tangents
c. Law of sines
d. Trigonometric functions

9. The _____ is the fraction of a complete cycle corresponding to an offset in the displacement from a specified reference point at time t = 0. Phase is a frequency domain or Fourier transform domain concept, and as such, can be readily understood in terms of simple harmonic motion. The same concept applies to wave motion, viewed either at a point in space over an interval of time or across an interval of space at a moment in time.
   a. Belt problem
   b. Best fit
   c. Bounded
   d. Phase of an oscillation or wave

10. In mathematics, a _____ decomposes a periodic function or periodic signal into a sum of simple oscillating functions, namely sines and cosines . The study of _____ is a branch of Fourier analysis. _____ were introduced by Joseph Fourier (1768-1830) for the purpose of solving the heat equation in a metal plate.
    a. Fourier series
    b. Belt problem
    c. Bounded
    d. Best fit

11. In mathematics, if f is a function from A to B then an _____ for f is a function in the opposite direction, from B to A, with the property that a round trip (a composition) from A to B to A (or from B to A to B) returns each element of the initial set to itself. Thus, if an input x into the function f produces an output y, then inputting y into the _____ f^{-1} (read f inverse, not to be confused with exponentiation) produces the output x. Not every function has an inverse; those that do are called invertible.
    a. Archimedes
    b. Prime number
    c. Inverse Function
    d. Maria Gaetana Agnesi

12. The _____ is a test to determine if a relation or its graph is a function or not. For a relation or graph to be a function, it can have at most a single y-value for each x-value. Thus, a vertical line drawn at any x-position on the graph of a function will intersect the graph at most once.

a. Vertical line test
b. Best fit
c. Bounded
d. Belt problem

13. In Euclidean geometry, a _____ is a straight curve. When geometry is used to model the real world, _____s are used to represent straight objects with negligible width and height. _____s are an idealisation of such objects and have no width or height at all and are usually considered to be infinitely long.
   a. Belt problem
   b. Line
   c. Best fit
   d. Bounded

14. In mathematics, the _____ or cyclometric functions are the so-called inverse functions of the trigonometric functions, though they do not meet the official definition for inverse functions as their ranges are subsets of the domains of the original functions. The principal inverses are listed in the following table.

If x is allowed to be a complex number, then the range of y applies only to its real part.

   a. Exsecant
   b. Exact constant expressions for trigonometric expressions
   c. Angle excess
   d. Inverse trigonometric functions

Chapter 5. IDENTITIES AND FORMULAS

1. In mathematics, the term _____ has several different important meanings:

   - An _____ is an equality that remains true regardless of the values of any variables that appear within it, to distinguish it from an equality which is true under more particular conditions. For this, the 'triple bar' symbol ≡ is sometimes used. (However, this can be ambiguous since the same symbol can also be used with different meanings, for example for a congruence relation.)
   - In algebra, an _____ or _____ element of a set S with a binary operation Â· is an element e that, when combined with any element x of S, produces that same x. That is, eÂ·x = xÂ·e = x for all x in S.
     - The _____ function from a set S to itself, often denoted id or id_S, is the function such that id(x) = x for all x in S. This function serves as the _____ element in the set of all functions from S to itself with respect to function composition.
     - In linear algebra, the _____ matrix of size n is the n-by-n square matrix with ones on the main diagonal and zeros elsewhere. This matrix serves as the _____ with respect to matrix multiplication.

A common example of the first meaning is the trigonometric _____

$$\sin^2 \theta + \cos^2 \theta = 1$$

which is true for all complex values of θ (since the complex numbers $\mathbb{C}$ are the domain of sin and cos), as opposed to

$$\cos \theta = 1,$$

which is true only for some values of θ, not all. For example, the latter equation is true when $\theta = 0$, false when $\theta = 2$

The concepts of 'additive _____' and 'multiplicative _____' are central to the Peano axioms. The number 0 is the 'additive _____' for integers, real numbers, and complex numbers. For the real numbers, for all $a \in \mathbb{R}$,

$$0 + a = a,$$

$$a + 0 = a, \text{ and}$$

$$0 + 0 = 0.$$

Similarly, The number 1 is the 'multiplicative _____' for integers, real numbers, and complex numbers.

a. Absolute value
b. Additive identity
c. Affinely extended real number system
d. Identity

Chapter 5. IDENTITIES AND FORMULAS

2. A _____ is an expression that compares quantities relative to each other. The most common examples involve two quantities, but any number of quantities can be compared. _____s are represented mathematically by separating each quantity with a colon, for example the _____ 2:3, which is read as the _____ 'two to three'.
   a. Best fit
   b. Belt problem
   c. Bounded
   d. Ratio

3. In mathematics, _____ are equalities that involve trigonometric functions that are true for every single value of the occurring variables. Geometrically, these are identities involving certain functions of one or more angles. These are distinct from triangle identities, which are identities involving both angles and side lengths of a triangle.
   a. Best fit
   b. Bounded
   c. Belt problem
   d. Trigonometric identities

Chapter 6. EQUATIONS

1. In mathematics, _____ is one of the basic operations defining a vector space in linear algebra Note that _____ is different from scalar product which is an inner product between two vectors.

More specifically, if K is a field and V is a vector space over K, then _____ is a function from K × V to V. The result of applying this function to c in K and v in V is denoted cv.

_____ obeys the following rules:

- Left distributivity:v = cv + dv;
- Right distributivity: c = cv + cw;
- Associativity:v = c;
- Multiplying by 1 does not change a vector: 1v = v;
- Multiplying by 0 gives the null vector: 0v = 0;
- Multiplying by -1 gives the additive inverse:v = -v.

Here + is addition either in the field or in the vector space, as appropriate; and 0 is the additive identity in either. Juxtaposition indicates either _____ or the multiplication operation in the field.

a. Bounded
b. Belt problem
c. Scalar multiplication
d. Best fit

2. Trigonometry is a branch of mathematics that deals with triangles, particularly those plane triangles in which one angle has 90 degrees (right triangles.) Trigonometry deals with relationships between the sides and the angles of triangles and with the _____ functions, which describe those relationships.

Trigonometry has applications in both pure mathematics and in applied mathematics, where it is essential in many branches of science and technology.

a. Best fit
b. Bounded
c. Trigonometric
d. Belt problem

3. In mathematics, _____ are a method of defining a curve using parameters. A simple kinematical example is when one uses a time parameter to determine the position, velocity, and other information about a body in motion.

Abstractly, a relation is given in the form of an equation, and it is shown also to be the image of functions from items such as R^n.

Chapter 6. EQUATIONS

  a. Belt problem
  b. Best fit
  c. Bounded
  d. Parametric equations

4. A _____, in mathematics, is a number comprising a real number part and an imaginary number part; it is normally written in the form a + bi, where a and b are real numbers, and i is the square root of minus one.

_____s are a field in mathematics, with specific notions of addition, subtraction, multiplication and division, satisfying certain axioms. These operations extend the corresponding operations on real numbers, mainly because the product of two imaginary numbers (or the square of one imaginary number) is a negative real number.

  a. Complex number
  b. Bounded
  c. Belt problem
  d. Best fit

5. A _____ is the curve defined by the path of a point on the edge of circular wheel as the wheel rolls along a straight line. It is an example of a roulette, a curve generated by a curve rolling on another curve.

The _____ is the solution to the brachistochrone problem (i.e. it is the curve of fastest descent under gravity) and the related tautochrone problem (i.e. the period of a ball rolling back and forth inside this curve does not depend on the ball's starting position.)

  a. Bounded
  b. Best fit
  c. Belt problem
  d. Cycloid

6. _____ was an Italian linguist, mathematician, and philosopher. Agnesi is credited with writing the first book discussing both differential and integral calculus. She was an honorary member of the faculty at the University of Bologna.
  a. Prime number
  b. Inverse function
  c. Maria Gaetana Agnesi
  d. Archimedes

7. In mathematics, the _____ , sometimes called the witch of Maria Agnesi is the curve defined as follows. The _____ with labeled points

Chapter 6. EQUATIONS 35

Starting with a fixed circle, a point O on the circle is chosen. For any other point A on the circle, the secant line OA is drawn.

a. Best fit
b. Belt problem
c. Bounded
d. Witch of Agnesi

36   Chapter 7. TRIANGLES

1. The _____, in trigonometry, is a statement about any triangle in a plane, and an analogous statement in spherical trigonometry about triangles on a sphere. Where the sides of the triangle are a, b and c and the angles opposite those sides are A, B and C, then the _____ states that:

$$\frac{a}{\sin A} = \frac{b}{\sin B} = \frac{c}{\sin C}.$$

The common value of these three fractions is the diameter of the triangle's circumcircle. The _____ is also sometimes stated as

$$\frac{\sin A}{a} = \frac{\sin B}{b} = \frac{\sin C}{c}.$$

This law is useful when computing the remaining sides of a triangle if two angles and a side are known, a common problem in the technique of triangulation.

    a. Proofs of trigonometric identities
    b. Law of sines
    c. Law of tangents
    d. Law of cosines

2. The _____ of an angle is the ratio of the length of the opposite side to the length of the hypotenuse. In our case

$$\sin A = \frac{\text{opposite}}{\text{hypotenuse}} = \frac{a}{h}.$$

Note that this ratio does not depend on size of the particular right triangle chosen, as long as it contains the angle A, since all such triangles are similar.

The cosine of an angle is the ratio of the length of the adjacent side to the length of the hypotenuse.

    a. Bounded
    b. Belt problem
    c. Best fit
    d. Sine

3. A _____ is one of the basic shapes of geometry: a polygon with three corners or vertices and three sides or edges which are line segments. A _____ with vertices A, B, and C is denoted ABC.

In Euclidean geometry any three non-collinear points determine a unique _____ and a unique plane (i.e. a two-dimensional Euclidean space.)

a. Belt problem
b. Best fit
c. Bounded
d. Triangle

4. _____ is the speed of an aircraft relative to the ground. It is the sum of the aircraft's true airspeed and the current wind and weather conditions; a headwind subtracts from the _____, while a tailwind adds to it. Winds at other angles to the heading will have components of either headwind or tailwind as well as a crosswind component.
   a. Bounded
   b. Best fit
   c. Belt problem
   d. Ground speed

5. In trigonometry, the _____ is a statement about a general triangle which relates the lengths of its sides to the cosine of one of its angles. Using notation as in Fig. 1, the _____ states that

$$c^2 = a^2 + b^2 - 2ab\cos(\gamma),$$

or, equivalently:

$$b^2 = c^2 + a^2 - 2ca\cos(\beta),$$

$$a^2 = b^2 + c^2 - 2bc\cos(\alpha),$$

$$\cos(\gamma) = \frac{a^2 + b^2 - c^2}{2ab},$$

$$\cos(\beta) = \frac{a^2 + c^2 - b^2}{2ca},$$

$$\cos(\alpha) = \frac{b^2 + c^2 - a^2}{2bc}.$$

Note that c is the side opposite of angle γ, and that a and b are the two sides enclosing γ.

Chapter 7. TRIANGLES

  a. Law of sines
  b. Law of tangents
  c. Proofs of trigonometric identities
  d. Law of cosines

6. The _____ of an angle is the ratio of the length of the adjacent side to the length of the hypotenuse. In our case

$$\cos A = \frac{\text{adjacent}}{\text{hypotenuse}} = \frac{b}{h}.$$

The tangent of an angle is the ratio of the length of the opposite side to the length of the adjacent side. In our case

$$\tan A = \frac{\text{opposite}}{\text{adjacent}} = \frac{a}{b}.$$

The remaining three functions are best defined using the above three functions.

  a. Best fit
  b. Belt problem
  c. Bounded
  d. Cosine

7. In mathematics, _____ is one of the basic operations defining a vector space in linear algebra Note that _____ is different from scalar product which is an inner product between two vectors.

More specifically, if K is a field and V is a vector space over K, then _____ is a function from K × V to V. The result of applying this function to c in K and v in V is denoted cv.

_____ obeys the following rules:

- Left distributivity:v = cv + dv;
- Right distributivity: c = cv + cw;
- Associativity:v = c;
- Multiplying by 1 does not change a vector: 1v = v;
- Multiplying by 0 gives the null vector: 0v = 0;
- Multiplying by -1 gives the additive inverse:v = -v.

Here + is addition either in the field or in the vector space, as appropriate; and 0 is the additive identity in either. Juxtaposition indicates either _____ or the multiplication operation in the field.

a. Belt problem
b. Best fit
c. Bounded
d. Scalar multiplication

8. In mathematics, a _____ in a normed vector space is a vector (often a spatial vector) whose length is 1 (the unit length.) A _____ is often denoted by a lowercase letter with a superscribed caret or 'hat', like this: $\hat{\imath}$.

In Euclidean space, the dot product of two _____s is simply the cosine of the angle between them.

a. Affinely extended real number system
b. Absolute value
c. Additive identity
d. Unit Vector

9. In mathematics, the _____ is an operation which takes two vectors over the real numbers R and returns a real-valued scalar quantity. It is the standard inner product of the orthonormal Euclidean space. It contrasts with the cross product which produces a vector result.
a. Best fit
b. Belt problem
c. Dot product
d. Bounded

10. In geometry and trigonometry, an _____ is the figure formed by two rays sharing a common endpoint, called the vertex of the _____ . The magnitude of the _____ is the 'amount of rotation' that separates the two rays, and can be measured by considering the length of circular arc swept out when one ray is rotated about the vertex to coincide with the other Where there is no possibility of confusion, the term '_____' is used interchangeably for both the geometric configuration itself and for its angular magnitude (which is simply a numerical quantity.)
a. Additive identity
b. Affinely extended real number system
c. Absolute value
d. Angle

11. In geometry, two lines or planes (or a line and a plane), are considered _____ to each other if they form congruent adjacent angles (an L-shape.) The term may be used as a noun or adjective. Thus, referring to Figure 1, the line AB is the _____ to CD through the point B. Note that by definition, a line is infinitely long, and strictly speaking AB and CD in this example represent line segments of two infinitely long lines.

a. Best fit
b. Belt problem
c. Bounded
d. Perpendicular

12. In mathematics, _____ are a non-commutative number system that extends the complex numbers. The _____ were first described by Irish mathematician Sir William Rowan Hamilton in 1843 and applied to mechanics in three-dimensional space. They find uses in both theoretical and applied mathematics, in particular for calculations involving three-dimensional rotations such as in three-dimensional computer graphics and epipolar geometry, although they have been superseded in many applications by vectors and matrices.
    a. Belt problem
    b. Best fit
    c. Bounded
    d. Quaternions

Chapter 8. COMPLEX NUMBERS AND POLAR COORDINATES

1. A _____, in mathematics, is a number comprising a real number part and an imaginary number part; it is normally written in the form a + bi, where a and b are real numbers, and i is the square root of minus one.

   _____s are a field in mathematics, with specific notions of addition, subtraction, multiplication and division, satisfying certain axioms. These operations extend the corresponding operations on real numbers, mainly because the product of two imaginary numbers (or the square of one imaginary number) is a negative real number.

   a. Best fit
   b. Belt problem
   c. Bounded
   d. Complex number

2. An _____, in mathematics, is a number in the form bi where b is a real number and i is the square root of minus one, known as the imaginary unit. _____s and real numbers may be combined as complex numbers in the form a + bi where a is the real part and bi is the imaginary part. _____s can therefore be thought of as complex numbers where the real part is zero.
   a. Additive identity
   b. Imaginary number
   c. Absolute value
   d. Affinely extended real number system

3. In mathematics, the _____ of a complex number z, is the second element of the ordered pair of real numbers representing z, i.e. if z = (x,y), or equivalently, z = x + iy, then the _____ of z is y. It is denoted by Im(z) or $\Im\{z\}$, where $\Im$ is a capital I in the Fraktur typeface. The complex function which maps z to the _____ of z is not holomorphic.
   a. Additive identity
   b. Absolute value
   c. Imaginary unit
   d. Imaginary part

4. In mathematics, the _____ of a complex number z, is the first element of the ordered pair of real numbers representing z, i.e. if z = (x,y), or equivalently, z = x + iy, then the _____ of z is x. It is denoted by Re{z} or $\Re\{z\}$, where $\Re$ is a capital R in the Fraktur typeface. The complex function which maps z to the _____ of z is not holomorphic.
   a. Real part
   b. Belt problem
   c. Best fit
   d. Bounded

5. In mathematics, _____ is one of the basic operations defining a vector space in linear algebra Note that _____ is different from scalar product which is an inner product between two vectors.

42 *Chapter 8. COMPLEX NUMBERS AND POLAR COORDINATES*

More specifically, if K is a field and V is a vector space over K, then _____ is a function from K × V to V. The result of applying this function to c in K and v in V is denoted cv.

_____ obeys the following rules:

- Left distributivity:v = cv + dv;
- Right distributivity: c = cv + cw;
- Associativity:v = c;
- Multiplying by 1 does not change a vector: 1v = v;
- Multiplying by 0 gives the null vector: 0v = 0;
- Multiplying by -1 gives the additive inverse:v = -v.

Here + is addition either in the field or in the vector space, as appropriate; and 0 is the additive identity in either. Juxtaposition indicates either _____ or the multiplication operation in the field.

a. Best fit
b. Belt problem
c. Bounded
d. Scalar multiplication

6. In mathematics, the _____ of a real number is its numerical value without regard to its sign. So, for example, 3 is the _____ of both 3 and −3.

The _____ of a number a is denoted by | a |.

a. Additive identity
b. Absolute value
c. Exponential Function
d. Absolute value

7. In mathematics, the _____s may be described informally in several different ways. The _____s include both rational numbers, such as 42 and −23/129, and irrational numbers, such as pi and the square root of two; or, a _____ can be given by an infinite decimal representation, such as 2.4871773339..., where the digits continue in some way; or, the _____s may be thought of as points on an infinitely long number line.

These descriptions of the _____s, while intuitively accessible, are not sufficiently rigorous for the purposes of pure mathematics.

Chapter 8. COMPLEX NUMBERS AND POLAR COORDINATES

a. Belt problem
b. Best fit
c. Real number
d. Bounded

8. Trigonometry is a branch of mathematics that deals with triangles, particularly those plane triangles in which one angle has 90 degrees (right triangles.) Trigonometry deals with relationships between the sides and the angles of triangles and with the _____ functions, which describe those relationships.

Trigonometry has applications in both pure mathematics and in applied mathematics, where it is essential in many branches of science and technology.

a. Trigonometric
b. Best fit
c. Bounded
d. Belt problem

9. In mathematics, the _____ system is a two-dimensional coordinate system in which each point on a plane is determined by a distance from a fixed point and an angle from a fixed direction.

The fixed point (analogous to the origin of a Cartesian system) is called the pole, and the ray from the pole with the fixed direction is the polar axis. The distance from the pole is called the radial coordinate or radius, and the angle is the angular coordinate, polar angle, or azimuth.

a. Bounded
b. Best fit
c. Belt problem
d. Polar coordinate

10. In informal usage, _____ systems can have singularities: these are points where one or more of the _____s is not well-defined. For example, the origin in the polar _____ system (r,θ) on the plane is singular, because although the radial _____ has a well-defined value (r = 0) at the origin, θ can be any angle, and so is not a well-defined function at the origin. The Cartesian _____ system in the plane.

The prototypical example of a _____ system is the Cartesian _____ system, which describes the position of a point P in the Euclidean space R^n by an n-tuple

$$P = (r_1, ..., r_n)$$

of real numbers

$r_1, ..., r_n$.

a. Bounded
b. Belt problem
c. Coordinate
d. Best fit

11. The mathematical concept of a _____ expresses the intuitive idea that one quantity completely determines another quantity A _____ associates a unique value for each input of a specified type. The argument and value may be real numbers, but they can also be elements from any given sets: the domain and codomain of the _____.
a. Bounded
b. Best fit
c. Function
d. Belt problem

12. The _____ is a test to determine if a relation or its graph is a function or not. For a relation or graph to be a function, it can have at most a single y-value for each x-value. Thus, a vertical line drawn at any x-position on the graph of a function will intersect the graph at most once.
a. Vertical line test
b. Bounded
c. Belt problem
d. Best fit

13. In Euclidean geometry, a _____ is a straight curve. When geometry is used to model the real world, _____s are used to represent straight objects with negligible width and height. _____s are an idealisation of such objects and have no width or height at all and are usually considered to be infinitely long.
a. Bounded
b. Line
c. Belt problem
d. Best fit

14. The terms '_____' and 'independent variable' are used in similar but subtly different ways in mathematics and statistics as part of the standard terminology in those subjects. They are used to distinguish between two types of quantities being considered, separating them into those available at the start of a process and those being created by it, where the latter (_____s) are dependent on the former (independent variables.)

Chapter 8. COMPLEX NUMBERS AND POLAR COORDINATES

The independent variable is typically the variable being manipulated or changed and the _____ is the observed result of the independent variable being manipulated.

a. Belt problem
b. Best fit
c. Bounded
d. Dependent variable

15. The terms 'dependent variable' and '_____' are used in similar but subtly different ways in mathematics and statistics as part of the standard terminology in those subjects. They are used to distinguish between two types of quantities being considered, separating them into those available at the start of a process and those being created by it, where the latter (dependent variables) are dependent on the former (_____s.)

The _____ is typically the variable being manipulated or changed and the dependent variable is the observed result of the _____ being manipulated.

a. Independent variable
b. Absolute value
c. Additive identity
d. Affinely extended real number system

16. In mathematics, if f is a function from A to B then an _____ for f is a function in the opposite direction, from B to A, with the property that a round trip (a composition) from A to B to A (or from B to A to B) returns each element of the initial set to itself. Thus, if an input x into the function f produces an output y, then inputting y into the _____ f^{-1} (read f inverse, not to be confused with exponentiation) produces the output x. Not every function has an inverse; those that do are called invertible.

a. Maria Gaetana Agnesi
b. Archimedes
c. Prime number
d. Inverse Function

17. _____ generally conveys two primary meanings. The first is an imprecise sense of harmonious or aesthetically pleasing proportionality and balance; such that it reflects beauty or perfection. The second meaning is a precise and well-defined concept of balance or 'patterned self-similarity' that can be demonstrated or proved according to the rules of a formal system: by geometry, through physics or otherwise.

Chapter 8. COMPLEX NUMBERS AND POLAR COORDINATES

   a. Symmetry
   b. Bounded
   c. Belt problem
   d. Best fit

18. An injective function is called an injection, and is also said to be a _____ function (not to be confused with _____ correspondence, i.e. a bijective function.)

A function f that is not injective is sometimes called many-to-one. (However, this terminology is also sometimes used to mean 'single-valued', i.e. each argument is mapped to at most one value.)

   a. Additive identity
   b. One-to-one function
   c. Absolute value
   d. One-to-one

19. An injective function is called an injection, and is also said to be a _____

A function f that is not injective is sometimes called many-to-one. (However, this terminology is also sometimes used to mean 'single-valued', i.e. each argument is mapped to at most one value.)

   a. One-to-one function
   b. Additive identity
   c. One-to-one
   d. Absolute value

20. In mathematics, the _____ is a test used to determine if a function is injective, surjective or bijective.

Chapter 8. COMPLEX NUMBERS AND POLAR COORDINATES

Suppose there is a function f : X → Y with a graph., and you have a horizontal line of X x Y :
$$y_0 \in Y, \{(x, y_0) : x \in X\} = (X \times y_0).$$

- If the function is injective, then it can be visualized as one whose graph is never intersected by any horizontal line more than once.
- If and only if f is surjective, any horizontal line will intersect the graph at least at one point (when the horizontal line is in the codomain.)
- If f is bijective, any line horizontal or vertical will intersect the graph at exactly one point. Note that as opposed to the injective function test, the bijective one demands that the function is to be continous at all points alongside both axis. So that there are no 'jumps' in the function. Ie f(x)= y = ax+b is valid over -n<x<=0 and then jumps to f(x) = ax+(b+1) 0<x<n where n tends to infinity.

This test is also used to find whether or not the inverse of the function is indeed a function as well. This is due to the reflective properties of the function over y=x.

a. Bounded
b. Best fit
c. Belt problem
d. Horizontal line test

21. The _____ is a function in mathematics that produces as its output the exponentiation of Euler's number (e) by a real input variable. The application of this function to a value x is written as exp(x.) Equivalently, this can be written in the form e^x, where e is the mathematical constant that is the base of the natural logarithm (approximately 2.71828182846) and that is also known as Euler's number.
   a. Absolute value
   b. Additive identity
   c. Affinely extended real number system
   d. Exponential Function

22. In mathematics, the _____ of a number to a given base is the power or exponent to which the base must be raised in order to produce the number.

For example, the _____ of 1000 to the base 10 is 3, because 3 is how many 10s you must multiply to get 1000: thus 10 × 10 × 10 = 1000; the base 2 _____ of 32 is 5 because 5 is how many 2s one must multiply to get 32: thus 2 × 2 × 2 × 2 × 2 = 32. In the language of exponents: 10^3 = 1000, so $\log_{10} 1000$ = 3, and 2^5 = 32, so $\log_2 32$ = 5.

a. Belt problem
b. Best fit
c. Logarithm
d. Bounded

23. Any formula written in terms of logarithms may be said to be in _____.

In contexts including complex manifolds and algebraic geometry, a logarithmic differential form is a 1-form that, locally at least, can be written

$$\frac{df}{f}$$

for some meromorphic function (resp. rational function) f.

a. Bounded
b. Best fit
c. Belt problem
d. Logarithmic form

24. In mathematics, the term _____ has several different important meanings:

- An _____ is an equality that remains true regardless of the values of any variables that appear within it, to distinguish it from an equality which is true under more particular conditions. For this, the 'triple bar' symbol ≡ is sometimes used. (However, this can be ambiguous since the same symbol can also be used with different meanings, for example for a congruence relation.)
- In algebra, an _____ or _____ element of a set S with a binary operation Â· is an element e that, when combined with any element x of S, produces that same x. That is, eÂ·x = xÂ·e = x for all x in S.
    - The _____ function from a set S to itself, often denoted id or id_S, is the function such that id(x) = x for all x in S. This function serves as the _____ element in the set of all functions from S to itself with respect to function composition.
    - In linear algebra, the _____ matrix of size n is the n-by-n square matrix with ones on the main diagonal and zeros elsewhere. This matrix serves as the _____ with respect to matrix multiplication.

A common example of the first meaning is the trigonometric _____

$$\sin^2 \theta + \cos^2 \theta = 1$$

which is true for all complex values of θ (since the complex numbers $\mathbb{C}$ are the domain of sin and cos), as opposed to

$$\cos\theta = 1,$$

which is true only for some values of θ, not all. For example, the latter equation is true when $\theta = 0$, false when $\theta = 2$

The concepts of 'additive _____' and 'multiplicative _____' are central to the Peano axioms. The number 0 is the 'additive _____' for integers, real numbers, and complex numbers. For the real numbers, for all $a \in \mathbb{R}$,

$$0 + a = a,$$

$$a + 0 = a, \text{ and}$$

$$0 + 0 = 0.$$

Similarly, The number 1 is the 'multiplicative _____' for integers, real numbers, and complex numbers.

a. Affinely extended real number system
b. Additive identity
c. Absolute value
d. Identity

25. The Richter magnitude scale, also known as the local magnitude (M_L) scale, assigns a single number to quantify the amount of seismic energy released by an earthquake. It is a base-10 logarithmic scale obtained by calculating the logarithm of the combined horizontal amplitude of the largest displacement from zero on a Wood-Anderson torsion seismometer output. So, for example, an earthquake that measures 5.0 on the _____ has a shaking amplitude 10 times larger than one that measures 4.0.
a. Best fit
b. Bounded
c. Belt problem
d. Richter scale

ANSWER KEY

Chapter 1
1. c   2. a   3. b   4. a   5. c   6. d   7. d   8. a   9. b   10. d
11. d   12. a   13. d   14. a   15. d   16. b   17. d   18. d   19. d   20. d
21. d   22. d   23. d   24. b   25. b   26. d   27. d   28. c   29. d   30. d
31. d   32. d

Chapter 2
1. a   2. d   3. d   4. d   5. a   6. d   7. d   8. d   9. b   10. d
11. c   12. b   13. d   14. c   15. d   16. d   17. d

Chapter 3
1. a   2. d   3. b   4. d   5. d   6. d   7. d   8. d   9. b   10. a
11. d   12. d   13. a   14. d   15. a   16. b   17. d   18. c   19. d   20. a
21. b

Chapter 4
1. b   2. d   3. d   4. d   5. d   6. d   7. c   8. d   9. d   10. a
11. c   12. a   13. b   14. d

Chapter 5
1. d   2. d   3. d

Chapter 6
1. c   2. c   3. d   4. a   5. d   6. c   7. d

Chapter 7
1. b   2. d   3. d   4. d   5. d   6. d   7. d   8. d   9. c   10. d
11. d   12. d

Chapter 8
1. d   2. b   3. d   4. a   5. d   6. d   7. c   8. a   9. d   10. c
11. c   12. a   13. b   14. d   15. a   16. d   17. a   18. d   19. a   20. d
21. d   22. c   23. d   24. d   25. d

0 3 8 3

www.ingramcontent.com/pod-product-compliance
Lightning Source LLC
Chambersburg PA
CBHW081219230426

43666CB00015B/2813